ABOUT THE BO

When first introduced, the limerick's folksy manner and twisty ending entertained and delighted audiences throughout medieval Western Europe. Before long its simple, humorous style appeared in Mother Goose nursery rhymes as well as several Shakespearean plays. However, it wasn't until the mid—19th century with writers and poets such as Edward Lear, Robert Louis Stevenson, and Mark Twain that the limerick achieved the popularity that granted it the strength to last right up to present times.

Although its reputation is somewhat soiled, often bringing a blush to the cheeks of proper European gentry, the limerick need not be off—colour in content. Surprisingly, most experts in the field of children's literature as well as work intended for much older folk agree that the funniest limericks are those with a "clean" message.

With that in mind, all of the limericks I've written in this collection are intended for a young audience. And what better way to entertain that group but to borrow the skillful hand of my son, Doug Desjardins and complement the written word with colourful illustrations.

While an effort has been made to honour the prescribed rhyme scheme (aabba) and line cadence, there may be slight fluctuations in line length. For example, the eight syllables in the first line of Zeke The Ostrich appear inconsistent with the nine syllables of the first line of The Cat & Toy. This need not be a major concern for over the years the limerick has endured considerable experimentation and adaptation. Some variations include the double limerick (10 lines), the extended limerick (six lines), and the truncated limerick (short last line).

Doug and I want to thank friends and family who have patiently listened to my, at times, awkward oral presentations, while at the same time, robustly encouraged the publication of this collection.

All the best,

Paul Desjardins

MW
BOOKS

Note for libraries: A catalogue record for this book is available from Library and Archives Canada at www.collectionscanada.gc.ca

ISBN: 978-0-9868776-7-4

A giraffe roamed the veldt in a muddle,

"Can't drink with long legs from this puddle."

Having run out of tricks,
He attempted the splits.

"Too close! Oh, my gosh! I'm in trouble!"

Upset that his work fell short of the mark,

A woodpecker vainly stabbed at the bark.

**As his misery soared,
He noticed the board.**

**Petrified Forest
National Park.**

One day a bold lion looked for

A lioness to impress with his **roar,**

Once agape, the poor cat

Inhaled a wee rat.

'Twas the squeak sent her laughing to the floor.

A move to the city looked bleak,

For a mild-mannered ostrich named Zeke.

Midst the bustle and clatter,
His nerves they did shatter,

From a head banged
and bruised
on concrete.

Aware 'tis no fun to be coy,

A duck flapped his wings as a ploy.

Yet his vibrant display ,

In the end could not sway

The crude heart of a plastic decoy.

Ending months in a snow-covered lair,

Emerged a hungry and far-sighted bear.

From ripping and clawing
To gashing and mauling,

The scarecrow took days to repair.

A fox on a mission most foul,

Stole the eggs from the nest of an owl.

In the midst of the stealing,

A claw sent him reeling.

And here we thought only wolves howl!

There once was a frog a weak gaper,

Took volumes of bugs just to sate her.

As much as she'd like,
To hit as they light,

Her tongue's firmly stuck to fly paper.

In the flight world the mantle of power
Cloaks the hummer, the bird of the hour.

Of course, he's no match,

Let's say, easy to catch

For the cat with the face of a flower.

When it comes to the hunt most attest

That the cat is supreme in this quest.

But the chase 'tis no joy,
When the mouse is a toy;

For the stuffing is hard to digest.

Harassed by two birds it is writ
That a llama on a plan he did hit:

With a grin two teeth short

He hacked up a large snort,

And doused the foul
pair with one spit.

Once a mosquitoe did claim,
To sing while gulping a vein.

In the midst of a ditty,

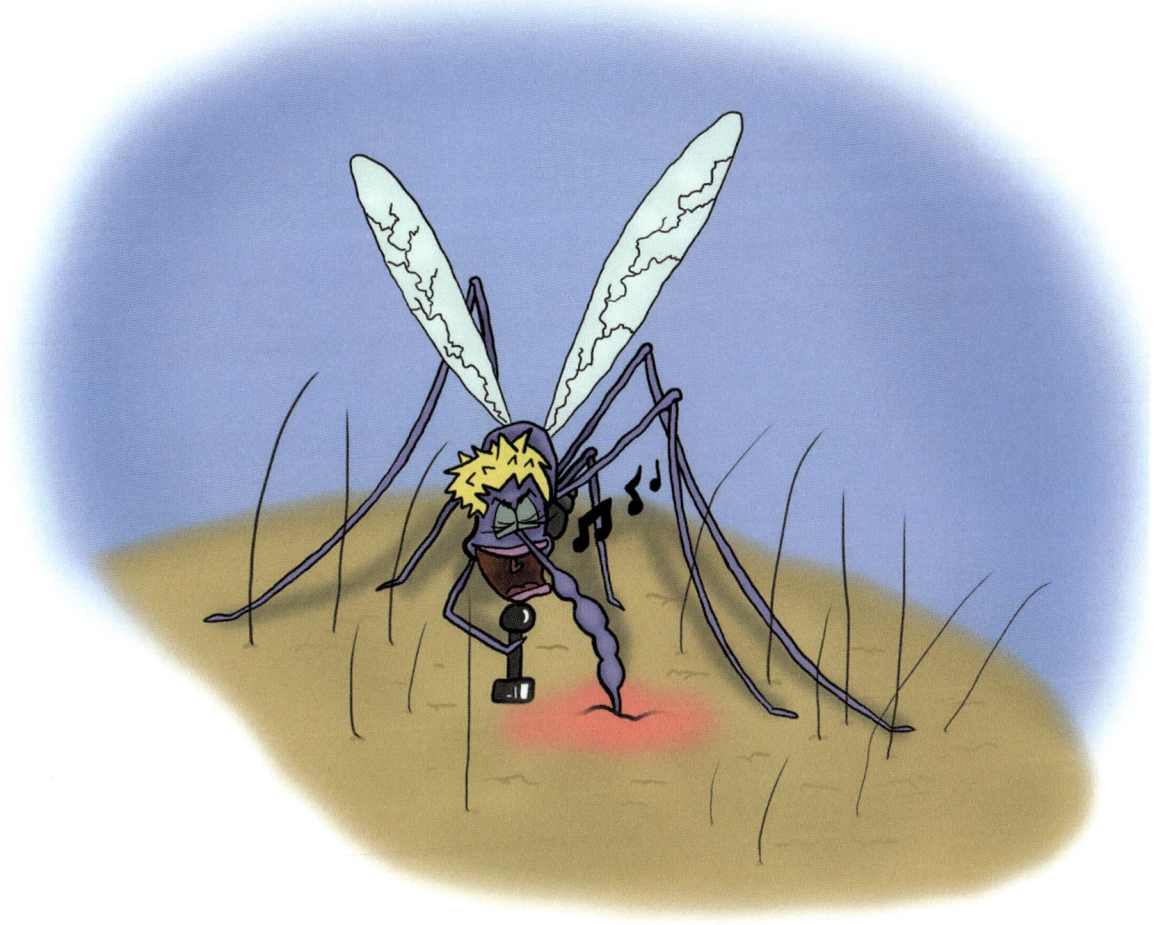

To her friends a real pity,

Caught a slap on the second refrain.

Once a blind diver named Pete,
A date with his girl he did keep.

With playful design,

Kissed a Great White's behind,
Under "Oops" Guinness mentions the feat.

A young monkey to his girl friend did boast,

"See that vine, I can swing farther than most."

In a bid to delight her,
Grabbed the tail of a viper,

His obit in the press she did post.

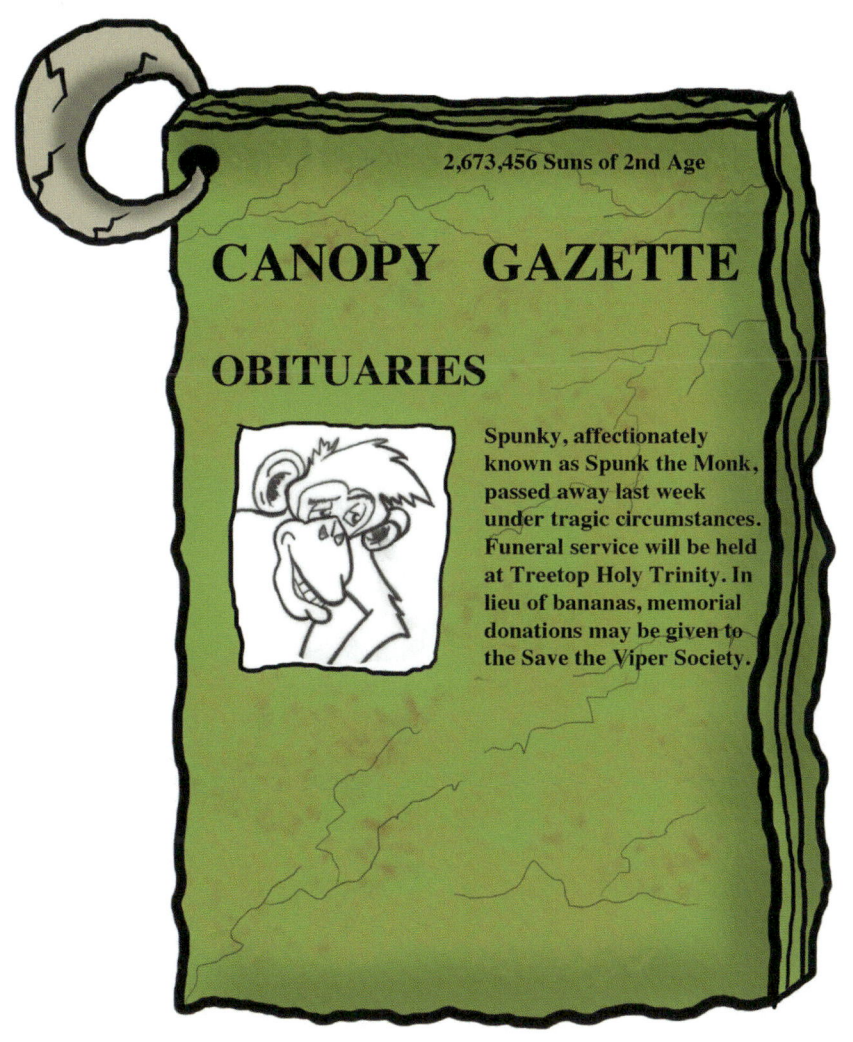

2,673,456 Suns of 2nd Age

CANOPY GAZETTE

OBITUARIES

Spunky, affectionately known as Spunk the Monk, passed away last week under tragic circumstances. Funeral service will be held at Treetop Holy Trinity. In lieu of bananas, memorial donations may be given to the Save the Viper Society.

There once was a snail named Stu,

Came down with a case of the flu.

Midst gasping and wheezes,
Then rasping and sneezes,

For every slip forward back two.

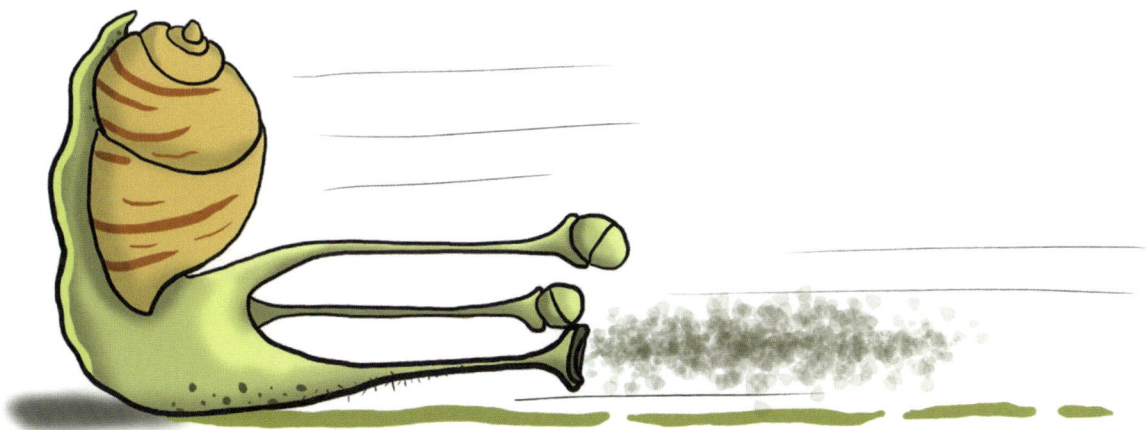

CPSIA information can be obtained
at www.ICGtesting.com
Printed in the USA
381259LV00002B/5

* 9 7 8 0 9 8 6 8 7 7 6 7 4 *